Coping With Grief

A handbook of proven techniques to help you overcome grief and start living again

Addison Cooper

Using This Book

Thank you for purchasing

Coping With Grief: A handbook of proven techniques to help you overcome grief and start living again.

This book was written for those who are grieving and for those who wish to help someone who is grieving. The book can be read from cover to cover or by just reading certain chapters of interest.

The book will give you effective and proven strategies to help you to come to terms with loss and to be able to start to rebuild your life so that you can, once again, engage in enjoyable and satisfying relationships and activities.

Please don't read it just once. Pick it up again from time to time and you will find that it helps you as your own perspective on grief changes over time.

There are more grief resources on my website **Coping With Grief**: https://www.copingwithgrief.net

There is a free 8 week Grief Help Course and there is also a free downloadable book about things that grievers should be particularly aware of.

I can be contacted through the website and you can subscribe for free to the grief newsletter which has articles and pre-release book extracts that are only available to subscribers. The newsletter is free of charge and is circulated every few weeks.

DEDICATION

For Celeste, Daniel and Milo.

Always with me, never parted.

Contents

Introduction

Losing someone you love is by far one of the most difficult and distressing experiences that you will ever encounter.

Death is not something that we talk about often, because it is not something that we experience often in these modern times, unlike our ancestors, whose life expectancy was much lower and to whom death was a more common occurrence.

Thanks to advances in modern medicine, losses are less frequent than in the past and usually occur later in our lives. Consequently, we don't have the same 'life experience' that our ancestors were able to rely on and so we feel unsure as to how to react when we are bereaved.

Sadly, though, we will all have to cope somehow when we are, one day, confronted with a loss.

Whether the loss is that of a parent, a sibling, a spouse, a friend or colleague, a pet, or the searing and unfathomable loss of a child, the process of grieving will provoke similar emotional, physical, behavioral, social and spiritual responses to varying degrees.

Despite the similar effects that grief has on us, no one person will experience the pain of loss in exactly the same way or to the same intensity. There is also a worrying lack of professional support services to help those who are grieving through this most difficult of times, so that they can process their grief, come to terms with their loss and rebuild their lives.

There are always platitudes and clichés that really don't help and can be a source of more pain and suffering. By trying to be kind, people often achieve the very opposite of what they intended. If you do find some support from family and friends, you often find that people are trying to fix you. The problem is, though, you don't need to be fixed. What you really need is a greater understanding of grief, what is happening to you, how grief runs its course, and what you can do to move forward.

This practical handbook has been written with the aim of making the process of grieving a little easier for those who are suffering the loss of a loved one or for those who would like to support someone they care about to pass through the pain of grief a little more quickly.

In this guide to coping with grief, we will look at the impact that grief has on the emotional, physical, behavioral, social and spiritual state of the bereaved individual and how these responses tend to manifest themselves.

Finally, this book will provide effective and proven strategies to help you to come to terms with your loss and to start to rebuild your life so that you can, once again, engage in pleasurable and satisfying relationships and activities.

Chapter One

WHAT IS GRIEF?

UNDERSTANDING GRIEF AND BEREAVEMENT

Grief is a natural and involuntary reaction to loss of any kind. It is often defined as 'intense sorrow', but it encompasses a whole multitude of emotions of widely varying intensities. There can be hurt, anger, bitterness, rage, fury, loneliness, regret, relief. Which emotions will show up, and the degree to which they will affect us, depends on the nature of the loss or upon 'who' is gone.

Grieving takes its time too. It is usually a long, elaborate, and intense process which hits us hard at first, then ebbs and flows, gets bogged down at times, meets dead-ends, and begins all over again, before finally reaching a resolution of sorts. It usually ends in accommodating and learning to live with the loss.

Grief is, in reality, a raw, animal activity. It can make us feel unhinged at times. We try to put a civilized veneer over it, but it will have its way with us, one way or another. Holding back grief is like damming up a stream, it causes it to become a river and when it bursts its bank, as, someday, it will, the consequences can be devastating.

The emotional reactions that grief sets in motion are often accompanied by changes in your sense of personal identity and in your relationships with others. You don't just recover from the loss; it changes you to some degree. This is the essence of bereavement.

Freud wrote, in a letter to his friend, the psychiatrist, Ludwig Binswanger, whose son had died:

"We know that the acute sorrow we feel after such a loss will run its course, but also that we will remain inconsolable, and will never find a substitute. No matter what may come to take its place, even should it fill that place completely, it yet remains something else.

And that is how it should be. It is the only way of perpetuating a love that we do not want to abandon."

Losses can range from the most significant event – the loss of a loved one – to other events such as a marriage breakup, loss of a job, retirement, loss of health or the death of a much-loved pet. Irrespective of the nature of the loss, if it was important to you then you will feel a sense of grief and that is completely normal.

Bereavement is the time that we spend in this process of grieving and mourning our loss.

There is no fixed time for how long this 'process' may take. For some people it may be a matter of weeks or months and for others it may be a year, two years, or more.

Mourning is not something that can be rushed. It is an important part of bereavement. If someone you loved died, then attending their funeral will be extremely stressful, but it does allow you to say goodbye and to bear witness to the reality of what has happened.

As distressing as it can be, we often feel the need to see evidence that a person has passed away before we can really begin the process of grieving properly.

Grief is not a medical condition either; it is a natural reaction to loss, but it can be likened to a physical injury. In many ways, the loss causes a mental wound, a laceration, that requires time to heal and to recover from.

It's our emotional response to grief that helps to promote the healing, and, although the event or person will remain in our memories forever, that raw pain and hurt at the shock of the initial loss will recede over time.

There is no right or wrong way to grieve

We all grieve in the manner in which we have lived. Emotionally expressive people become more expressive, while people who don't usually show feelings openly may become even more constrained. Problems occur when other people try to push us into behaving in ways that are comfortable for them, and not necessarily expressive of who we are. When a person who is normally quite open and expressive of their emotions is compelled to restrain them, they may later experience physical symptoms or even illness as a result.

There are several key points to remember:

It is normal and healthy for you to feel and express intense and painful emotions when grieving a significant loss.

Expressions of grief will help you to learn to live with your loss.

It is normal to experience a wide range of emotions—shock, sadness, yearning, loneliness, anger, anguish, guilt, despair, as well as relief, hope, acceptance and accommodation.

You will not grieve in stages, despite what others may say—grief is not linear. It is a roller coaster, chaotic, 'all over the place' kind of experience.

Painful feelings will decrease in intensity over time if you receive the right kind of support.

If the intensity of your feelings does not decrease after a significant period; it could be a sign that professional help is needed.

If you hold your grief in, find it difficult to express it in an outward, observable manner, that can also be a sign of the need for professional help.

Bereaved people who have not been able to express grief in ways that are best for them are highly likely to be more vulnerable to physical and psychological illness in the long term.

Chapter Two

WHAT IS 'COPING'?

Coping is about dealing with and trying to overcome problems and difficulties. Unfortunately, though, in grief, we are often judged on just how well we are dealing with and overcoming our problems and difficulties. There are always people who will make comments about a grieving person like 'They seem to be coping well with their loss', or 'They aren't coping well at all with their loss'. These people are usually, consciously or unconsciously, judging your wellbeing on how they, themselves, feel about what you are doing. They usually imagine themselves in your position and imagine how they would cope and are then quite happy to measure how you are handling your emotions as opposed to how they imagine they would handle their emotions under the same circumstances.

Bereaved people are usually aware that they are being judged and find themselves walking a grief tightrope as they try to come to terms with their loss. If you are visibly distressed and crying, you know that you will likely be described as 'not coping very well'. Grieving people spend a lot of time apologizing to others for crying so publicly. If you keep your outward expression to a minimum, then you know that you will likely be described as 'coping very well', even though it may be extremely difficult and distressing to deny yourself the opportunity to express your pain to others. And, of course, we all know that you must be careful not to be seen as coping 'too well' because if you don't cry and don't appear to be filled with sorrow or pain, then there is the very real possibility that you could be described as being 'cold'. There's a fine line to walk in the way that we express our grief if we wish to meet other people's expectations. In grief counseling we sometimes talk about 'the grief police' as a way of describing society's expectations of the bereaved.

My motivation for writing this book was, in part, to outline what coping really is. Quite frankly, when we are newly bereaved, we are 'coping' if we manage to simply show up each day. Each morning that you get out of bed, dress yourself, put one foot in front of the other and manage to carry out essential tasks, you are coping! You probably do this on auto pilot, but it's still coping. At first, we all just do our best to survive something that feels as though it can't actually be survived.

It doesn't help, either, to draw comparisons of who is worse off in grief. Grief is an entirely subjective experience. There's no comfort in being told that there is someone who is worse off than you. We can only feel our own pain. If I have a terrible toothache, I find it difficult to take comfort from being told that someone else has a worse one! Unfortunately, again, in grief, there are plenty of people who will compare your loss with the losses that others have suffered. It's that common trait of judging how your coping measures up to how you're expected to cope.

The thing is, people are often intolerant of strong reactions to pain. After a very short time, even after a sudden or traumatic death, you can find yourself on the receiving end of the usual, well worn, clichés like "come on, buck up", "being sad will just make you feel worse", "every cloud has a silver lining", "you need to think of the kids", "perhaps it was God's will", "he/she is in a better place now", "they wouldn't want you to be upset", "they would want you to find happiness again", "you're still young—you could always have another baby", "someone else will come along", "you can get married again...". They will say anything they can think of to placate your feelings.

Although these platitudes and clichés are expressed out of concern and a genuine belief that getting distressed is bad for you, they serve to, consciously or unconsciously, stop you from expressing your feelings in the manner that is best for you. When we express our feelings, we are seen as calling for help, which can embarrass people, or make them feel inadequate, even though they want to help. For some, though, they just want you to stop signaling for help as they simply don't want to be available. When we apologize for getting upset, we are often apologizing for choosing them to comfort us.

Showing constant distress can also get you labeled as 'falling apart', 'breaking down', 'losing it', 'cracking up' or 'not coping'. You may even think of yourself in these terms if you feel that you are not showing enough self-control. These terms, however, are demeaning, disparaging, condescending and patronizing. They show a complete lack of understanding of the nature and process of grief.

Showing stoical restraint, on the other hand, when someone you love has died, will get you labeled as being 'strong', 'brave', 'courageous', someone who is 'holding themselves together' or is 'coping well'. These expressions are all examples of how we use language to prevent or control how people express their feelings.

Maybe it's the raw crudity of the emotions of grief that explains why we so often find its expression to be embarrassing in ourselves and in others. We normally go to great lengths to present ourselves as being competent and responsible, but in grief our 'adultness' is pushed aside by such overwhelming primitive feelings; it ignites the fear of being out of control – we, and others, are shocked by the prospect of chaos.

The only way we can begin the process of 'curing' our grief is by recognising, admitting and describing our loss and by examining all the parts of our life that were touched by the deceased person so that we can, over time, manage the toughest balancing act there is; that of both letting go and also holding on.

Chapter Three

THE COMMON TRAITS OF GRIEF

G rief affects people in different ways and to different degrees. Each individual person grieves in their own unique way because human beings are unique in their own particular way and will react differently to different events.

Your reaction to loss is determined, to a large extent, by the relationship you had with the person who died and by your unique personality and your unique life experiences.

How you express your grief is affected by your upbringing, your cultural expectations and etiquette, your religion, if you are religious, the influences of your family and community, and by how you, yourself, view death.

Regardless, though, there are many common traits which, although they can be quite worrying, are perfectly normal, and are all part of the grieving process. The way in which grief manifests itself can be broadly divided into physical, emotional, behavioral, social and spiritual in nature.

Physical expressions of grief often include a multitude of reactions such as crying, sighing, headaches, stomach aches, heart flutters, frequent yawning, loss of appetite or increased appetite, difficult in sleeping or oversleeping, restlessness or lethargy, irritability, aches, pains and muscular tension.

Emotional expressions of grief include feeling depressed, longing, yearning, sadness, feelings of fear, anxiety, hopelessness, frustration, panic, anger or guilt. These, and many more, are all normal emotions following loss. You may, for instance, be angry at the hospital staff for their perceived failings in saving your loved one, or you may be angry at God for allowing your loved one to be taken from you. You may feel intense guilt and blame yourself following a suicide, and you may regret things that you said or failed to say to them before they died. These are just a few of the common emotions following a bereavement.

Behavioral expressions of grief include withdrawing from others or the outside world, lacking energy to engage in enjoyable activities, losing interest in eating or being social, becoming more irritable, impatient or angry. Other common expressions can include restlessness and excessive activity, limited ability to control unwanted behaviors causing poor dietary choices, forgetting to exercise, and indulging in overeating, smoking, and overconsumption of caffeine. This kind of change in behavior can further exacerbate the effects of grief and make them more noticeable.

Social expressions of grief are often tied in with behavioral expressions, as feeling isolated and lonely and preferring to keep your own company creates difficulty in engaging in any meaningful conversations with other people. If you usually enjoy the company of others, you may now find yourself feeling detached from the world, cut off from family, friends, and your community, feeling limited or having no interest in those around you.

Spiritual or religious expressions of grief can include questioning your faith or beliefs and struggling to understand the reason for your loss and suffering. You may begin to challenge the purpose of life and the meaning of death.

Other traits of grief include forgetfulness, difficulty focusing, and constantly changing your mind. If your concentration has suffered lately and you find it difficult to make a decision or to plan anything, what you are experiencing is completely normal. Rest assured that all the grief expressions mentioned above are completely normal adaptive reactions and form part of the process of grieving a loss.

Please try not to make any major life-changing decisions, if you can, until you are further along in your grief. It is usually advised that for at least a year after your loss, you refrain from making any major decisions, if you can. Put them off for a while, as you may not be in the right frame of mind to be making decisions that can have a huge impact on the rest of your life. If you really must, consider discussing your options with someone you can trust, such as a close friend or look for professional advice.

Chapter Four

THE WAVELIKE PATTERN OF GRIEF

Psychologists, psychiatrists and psychotherapists have been studying grief for a very long time and they have treated, spoken to and interviewed hundreds of thousands of grievers during that time. The conclusion is that there is a common journey that most of us will experience as we progress through our grief.

The first reaction to loss usually includes some or all of the following: shock, disbelief, confusion, sadness, yearning, pining, longing, loneliness, despair, helplessness, guilt, fear, lethargy, physical distress, separation anxiety, obsessive dwelling on the past and apprehension about the future, regret, remorse, or sorrow for what has befallen us. Sleep disorders, eating irregularities, physical ailments, anxiety, anger, and depression are all common conditions following a bereavement.

Grief involves painfully reorganizing and adjusting to a world without our loved one in it, and it is this change and adaptation to our new circumstances that is what we call 'grieving'.

In the early days it can be all-consuming, completely overwhelming and debilitating, but, over time, most people experience periods of semi normality broken up by less frequent and less intense periods of grief as it settles to a subconscious level where it sits, in the background, only occasionally producing moments of stronger, more noticeable thoughts and feelings about the person who died.

The wavelike pattern of grief

It is very helpful to think of grief as following a wavelike pattern. For most people, in the immediate aftermath of loss, the waves are very intense and come at us thick and fast, not allowing us much of a break in between them. For some, though, the individual waves are quite gentle at first, rising to a peak over the following few months as the reality of the death sinks in.

For the majority, as time moves on, the waves of grief hit a little less hard and a little less often. Unfortunately, for a small percentage of grievers, there isn't much variation in the intensity of the waves as time goes on. The rhythm and pace of grief differs from person to person.

Most people's experience of grief is that the break between each wave gets longer, and they think that things are getting better. Often, though, an unexpectedly big wave can hit again, and it will seem, for a time, that things are getting worse. There is always a trigger that causes these large waves, whether we are aware of it or not.

Triggers can be anything from a significant date, like an anniversary or a birthday, to hearing a shared favorite song on the radio, catching the whiff of a significant favorite food, the changing of the seasons, glimpsing a stranger who looks like a lost loved one or reminiscing about what you were doing this time last year. The triggers may not be obvious, as they often occur at a subconscious level, but if you can identify them, you will be better prepared for them next time.

Thinking about grief as a series of waves with different triggers helps to illustrate the differences between people's grief and to explain why some people seem to struggle more than others, and why grief can seem to intensify after a period of feeling better.

Knowing that your grief will follow a wavelike pattern helps you to be more prepared if your grief suddenly intensifies. If you come to expect these ups and downs, to understand that grief is a sequence of good days and bad days, with mostly bad days at first, then an equal number of good and bad, finally giving way to mostly good days, then you will be less likely to think that you are getting worse each time you experience a difficult day.

It can help you to feel more in control if you understand what to expect, and this may help your grieving process. No one else's grief will follow the exact same pattern as yours, though, because your experience and your triggers are unique to you and the relationship you had with the deceased.

Over time, you will learn to adapt to the emotions of grief when they arrive, as they will, from time to time. You move on from believing that you will never get through this, to thinking that you really hate this, to finally understanding that, although you do not want this and you still hate it, you will get through it, like you have done so many times before.

It's not necessarily that the intensity of grief changes over time, it's that your relationship to that intensity changes over time, with experience.

Feeling moments of grief years after your loss should not make you doubt whether you have really adapted to the loss because experiencing the emotion is a part of loving someone, a reminder that you never stopped loving them, the emotion itself is different to the process of adapting to the emotion.

The thing is, loss is permanent, and so too, in that case, is our grief, because our grief is our ongoing response to our loss. We can and should expect it to surge and then recede, as we alternate between experiencing the pain of the loss, and then being able to set it aside for a while.

Experiencing the loss, gradually, over time, gives way to being able to finally set it aside. Grief is a very inconsistent experience, not a uniform one. There is always a powerful response to the fact that someone we love died, but it changes in how it feels over time, allowing us to integrate and accommodate our loss and be able to move on. We adapt.

Chapter Five

PHYSICAL REACTIONS TO GRIEF

Physical reactions

G rief is often experienced physically, it resides in our bodies, not just our minds. There are a multitude of intense physical reactions to loss, all of them initiated to bring the pain of loss down to a manageable level. When someone we love dies, our body produces several chemicals that are like morphine, called endogenous opioids, also known as endorphins. They are nature's painkillers. They are there to help us through the shock of loss, and they are responsible for the numbing feeling that most of us experience at the beginning of our grief.

For those of us who cry, these chemicals are released in tears. Crying releases both oxytocin and those endogenous opioids. These feel-good chemicals help to ease both physical and emotional pain, which is why it is particularly important for other people not to try to prevent crying. These soothing chemicals are also released through physical exercise, providing another form of release for those who find it difficult to cry.

Gradually, though, as the weeks go by, the production of these chemicals decreases and around four to six weeks later their production is significantly lower. Around this time, our increased distress causes a greater awareness of the reality of the death, and the body attempts (through increased crying) to produce more chemicals to help us to survive the impact of this awful realization.

Crying works. Crying copiously works even better. Don't hold back the tears of grief, let them flow. How often have you sat down, had a good cry, and felt better afterwards? It is important for people who are supporting you to understand the benefit of crying, and not try to stop it. It is also important to be kind to yourself—to let go of your need to be in control and just surrender to the urge to cry those healing tears.

Not eating, not sleeping

Not eating and not sleeping are common occurrences in grief and are nothing to worry about in the first few weeks following a loss. The chemicals produced by the body, those opioids that help to soften the impact of grief in the early weeks, can also have a relaxing effect on some of your muscles, including those used for digestion. Because these muscles are slowed down, the body tells itself not to eat because it may struggle to eliminate the waste.

Our bodies, at this time, do not need the same amount of food that they normally would, and the stress of grief activates our body's stress response system, also known as the fight or flight response, which reduces our appetite to allow energy to be redirected to the muscles involved in fight or flight.

The most important thing, at this time, is that the food we eat is nutritious and easily digested. Fresh fruit and vegetables, in small quantities, are especially helpful.

One of the main reasons for not sleeping, is the amount of adrenaline that is produced by grief that stays trapped in our bodies. Adrenaline is the stress hormone produced when we perceive a threat, and the impact of grief is perceived as a threat to us by our subconscious mind. It is produced to prepare us for fight or flight. Bereavement and trauma are, clinically, regarded as the most potent forms of stress that the body has to endure, so we produce enormous amounts of adrenaline to help us to 'cope'. Our muscles, charged with adrenaline, become tense and contracted. Our heart (myocardium, the muscular layer of the heart) becomes strained and beats more rapidly, producing heart palpitations that ready us for action.

But, despite this ancient defense mechanism firing up to protect us, nothing, physically, happens and we are left primed, just in case, making it difficult to sleep.

Interestingly, in previous generations, and still today, in some cultures, we would have used a significant amount of adrenaline in the grieving process. In the past, intense mournful wailing after a death, often at a funeral or wake, would continue for two or three days and nights by a family or cultural group, at the end of which time exhaustion would take over and adrenaline would no longer be present.

As well as adrenaline, there is another hormone called cortisol that is produced by the body's response to stress, and it makes us feel very uncomfortable. Many bereaved people find themselves turning to drugs or using alcohol to help with the discomfort of the adrenaline and cortisol, and to help them sleep, whereas they would be better off burning off these stress hormones by going for a long walk, or to the gym, or by playing an outdoor sport, preferably in the company of a friend who will allow them to talk about whatever is on their mind at the time.

Other activities that can help are gardening, household chores, cleaning and tidying up, mowing the lawn, painting the fence, washing the car and many more simple activities.

Many of my clients find that a massage helps when they are feeling distressed. Massages relax tight muscles and are well known for precipitating crying. They allow us to feel nurtured. Look for a masseur who won't try to 'counsel' you or to 'fix things' at the same time.

Bodily distress

Any bodily system can be affected by grief and the effects can be surprising, ranging from mild to severe. You might experience skin eruptions, or gastrointestinal disturbances like heartburn, dyspepsia, constipation or diarrhea. You might experience more severe effects such as chest pain, muscle spasms or blinding headaches. A well-documented phenomenon of bereavement is the experience of symptoms that mimic symptoms of the person who died, or manifestations of what were imagined symptoms that they might have experienced.

I have counseled several people who have experienced severe chest pain after they lost someone who died from a heart attack. I have even helped a lady who developed a limp after her husband died. Her husband had needed a walking stick in his final year before his death. No obvious medical reason could be found for my client's limp, but it went away after a few sessions that involved grief counseling and some hypnotherapy.

Whenever unusual physical symptoms appear after bereavement it is especially important to have them checked medically first, before seeking counseling or some other form of mental health therapy. It isn't necessarily 'all in the mind' following bereavement.

Chapter Six

EMOTIONAL REACTIONS TO GRIEF

There are many emotional reactions to loss. Some are to be expected, some can be surprising, some are transient, some can cause very real concern. Sadness, longing, pining, yearning, depression, anguish, guilt, are just some of the kinds of emotions that are commonly associated with grief. Depression is understandably common following bereavement but so too is anger, guilt and the desire to replace that which has been lost. Depression and despair can become seriously debilitating for some grievers, taking root in their life and not wanting to leave.

Depression

In clinical practice we use the word depression to describe a psychiatric condition for which there is known treatment, usually prescription medication combined with a talking therapy (counseling, psychotherapy, hypnotherapy). Whilst the experience of grief may seem to be the same as clinical depression, there are differences. Clinical depression involves the way we think, while grief involves the way we feel. Profound sadness is a more appropriate way of describing grief, or 'feeling' depressed rather than 'being' depressed. Experiencing profound sadness or 'feeling' depressed does not necessarily require prescription medication. The best treatment for profound sadness is to have a friend or family member willing to listen to you as you retell and re-describe what happened and how you feel about it, again and again, from slightly different angles, crying whenever the need arises, without embarrassment or fear of being judged. Coping with grief comes from understanding who you are and all that you have been, and being able to express how you feel, unfettered by social conventions, it doesn't come from a medical prescription for an externally applied drug.

Grief is very regularly, and very easily, confused with clinical depression. For example; persistent feelings of sadness or hopelessness, unaccounted increases or decreases in appetite, diminished pleasure or interest in activities, insomnia or hypersomnia, bouts of weeping and sadness, fatigue, persistent agitation, excessive guilt, an inability to concentrate, recurrent thoughts of death, and occasional expressions of 'I wish I was dead', look and sound like clinical depression and can scare those who care about the bereaved into pushing them to prematurely look for medical help, to get a prescription for 'something'. Before doing this, it may be wise to see a professional bereavement counselor who should be able to carry out a grief assessment and explain the difference between clinical depression and profound sadness.

Major depressive disorders are not characterized by the waves, or roller coaster, of ups and downs normally experienced in grief, but by a persistent feeling of sadness and hopelessness that is unremitting after more than two weeks. These reactions can be so severe that they impair your ability to function at home, work, or school. If this is the case, then medical help may well be the best course of action.

It is worth remembering that in our grief we may experience feelings of emptiness or despair that seem like they will never lift. This is not a sign that we are mentally ill but an entirely appropriate reaction to an acute loss. Feeling depressed, or appearing profoundly sad, after a loss is often viewed as an aberration rather than a natural response, prompting well-intentioned friends and relatives to try to talk us out of it. But it is an entirely normal reaction, and encouragement to snap out of it from others is not helpful during this period. To not experience any depression or deep sadness after the passing of a loved one would, in fact, be considered highly unusual.

If grieving is the process of adapting to loss, then feeling depressed, feeling inconsolable at times, is a step along the path to recovery and to rebuilding your life. As you start to adjust to life without your loved one, your life begins to become a little calmer and more peaceful. Your physical symptoms alleviate, and your depressive feelings begin to recede.

Over time, you begin to live and to feel present again, but you cannot do so until you have given grief the time it needs to run its course.

Anger

Anger is a common, often confusing or surprising reaction to loss. Anger is a primitive defensive response. We absolutely need anger as part of our survival instinct, but it can be intense and frightening to ourselves or others. It may surface as a result of the nature of the death, perhaps the suddenness, or perceived preventability. It may also result from the kind of behavior that the deceased showed prior to death—for example, risk-taking, drug use, drunkenness, rebelliousness or plain carelessness. There may have been medical mismanagement or neglect, or we might believe that was the case and project our feelings of guilt or regret onto another.

Anger is felt by both men and women, but is more likely to be expressed by men, and is usually most apparent around the time of the news of the death or when the numbness begins to subside, even if only momentarily. Unfortunately, though, anger may be directed towards those who are closest—family and friends, or a previously trusted medical carer or team.

The immense stress of grief is perceived, subconsciously, as a threat. We react as though in a hostile environment and anger is our most primitive self defense mechanism that is activated to be able to defend ourselves, our family and our community. Anger goes hand in hand with the fight or flight response when experiencing extreme stress. It is natural and understandable, but it can isolate you at a time when you most need support. It can drive away the very people you need most.

So how should you deal with the anger? The first thing to do is to explore it. When do you get angry? What seems to trigger it? Is your anger proportional to the cause of the anger? How do you express it? What does it do to others?

After exploring these questions, you may find that your anger is not really focused on any responsible person or perceived injustice. You may realize that most times you are not angry at an individual. You are angry at your own grief, loss, and isolation. The root of the word bereaved means to have something taken away from you—forcibly. Someone you love and care about was taken away from you and there is nothing you can do about it. Who wouldn't be angry at that?

The best way to deal with anger is to channel it. Sometimes physical exercise can help you to cope. Activities like sport, gardening, running or housework. Punching bags work well too, as does hitting a big old tyre with a hammer, chopping wood, or smashing up old crockery. Also helpful is to write a letter (and not send it), talk about your feelings, take a car ride with the music turned up and scream as loud as you can, or find an empty beach and scream into the sea. Fantasies can be an effective way to cope with anger too, for example, imagining what you would tell your loved one if you met them in a future afterlife. You do not need to believe in an afterlife for this to be helpful. A client of mine once told me; "I told her what her death did to me. How hard it is without her. How I wish she had taken better care of her health. But I came to realize that she couldn't have known. It wasn't her fault. I've been so angry at her for leaving me, but it wasn't her fault. I'm not angry at her anymore."

Anger must be expressed somehow or it can build up on the inside and explode at inappropriate moments or cause physical symptoms later on like those described earlier.

Aggression is not anger. Aggression is hostile or violent behavior, a readiness to attack or to confront another person. Bereavement does not make people aggressive. Aggression is a personality trait that was already present before the bereavement. No one should have to be on the receiving end of aggression, no matter how much the grieving person is hurting. It is important not to confuse raised voices, angry words, screaming or shouting, or the expressive hitting of inanimate objects, with aggression. The intensity of anger experienced in grief can be frightening and unfamiliar to the bereaved person and to those supporting them, but it is really another way of expressing terrible pain.

Guilt

Guilt is one of the most common, and crippling of unexpected emotions. Guilt is corrosive. It affects physical and psychological health. It eats us up from the inside, creating pain, and producing disturbing memories. There are several different types of guilt.

There is the guilt that we feel when we believe we contributed to the death because of something we did or something we failed to do. For example, what if we had taken the person to a doctor or recognized a symptom? The death could have been avoided. What if you couldn't convince your spouse to stop drinking or smoking and their drinking or smoking caused or contributed to their death? There are many people who have died from lung cancer or cirrhosis of the liver who still couldn't stop smoking or drinking even after their diagnosis, no matter what the family did to try to encourage them to give it up. We can still feel guilty even though we could not really control their actions.

We might see our loss as being a punishment for something we have done. In working with the bereaved I have had my clients confess to all kinds of wrongdoing, like criminal acts, spiteful acts, selfish acts, lustful or covetous thoughts, infidelity, not attending their place of worship or praying to God often enough. They all believed that their acts may have been responsible for the death of their loved one.

Perhaps we feel that we could have been a better parent, better brother or sister, son, or daughter. We may wish we could turn back the clock and do or say things differently.

I have lost count of the number of bereaved people who have told me how guilty they felt about the years they missed through falling out with someone and not speaking to them until they learned of a terminal diagnosis, or worse, learned that the person had died. Many come to regret all those lost years.

We may ask ourselves "Why them and not me?". We wonder why we are alive when someone else died. This is particularly common with siblings when a brother or sister dies, especially if the deceased was the parent's favorite. The surviving siblings can easily believe that it is they who should have died instead. Older people feel this guilt when someone younger dies and they believe that they should have died instead.

We may feel guilty or ashamed of how badly we seem to be coping with our loss or we may think we are doing too well. Or we may experience both of those emotions. Imagine trying to join in a celebration for the rest of the family's sake, whilst feeling ashamed of even trying such a thing after losing your spouse, only to find yourself enjoying the celebration and then feeling guilty at enjoying yourself so soon after your loss.

As bereaved people, we may wish we could turn back the clock, do something differently, do more, say less, prevent the death from occurring, no matter how unrealistic that wish may be. By running through these scenarios in our heads, imagining doing things differently we give ourselves another opportunity to express our love, another way of saying 'there is nothing I wouldn't have done to keep this person alive'.

When we feel guilt or shame, we need a compassionate friend or family member to simply listen to us when we say that we wish we had just one more time to say, 'I love you', or to say how sorry we are for our perceived transgressions. We need the person listening to us to not try to make us feel better, to not try to take our guilt away. For those trying to help the bereaved, words like 'Come on, you mustn't blame yourself', 'It wasn't your fault' or 'He/she wouldn't want you to blame yourself' are more irritating than helpful. Just let us say what we need to say and feel what we need to feel.

Identify your guilt, examine it. Where is it coming from? Is it realistic? We often hold unrealistic expectations of what we can control or accomplish. The truth is, there are many things we cannot control.

Ask yourself: Given the circumstances, what could you have done differently? What has the experience taught you? Sometimes we gain perspective on our guilt by simply reflecting on the question, "Would other people find me guilty?" "Would I be so hard on someone I know and care about under the same circumstances?" If you still feel guilty over something you did, or didn't do, said or didn't say, you may want to write a letter to the person you lost and perhaps read it at their grave site, or even talk to an empty chair while pretending the person is sitting in it (a highly effective technique from a form of therapy known as Gestalt Therapy). It may seem strange at first, but it is an enormously powerful form of self-help therapy.

The hole in the soul

Grief is very often experienced as a void, an emptiness, a profound absence of a person's presence - "like part of me has gone", "like a part of me died when she/he died", which can lead some to believe that the remedy for the pain of grief is to fill that void again, to replace what was lost. There is often advice from well-meaning family and friends about how "you're still young enough to..." marry again if a partner has died or have another baby if the loss was the result of a miscarriage, a stillbirth, a neonatal death, or the death of a young child. It is usually best to completely ignore this kind of advice, well intentioned as it may be, and, where possible, avoid making major decisions in the first twelve to eighteen months. Major decisions would include selling the family home, remarrying, becoming pregnant again, changing jobs or ending friendships.

In the days, weeks and months following loss, nothing can really fill that emotional void. It can, however, be of significant help if family and friends can provide some of the important things that are now absent after the loss. Love, friendship, affection, physical touch (when non-exploitative and appropriate), money, emotional support, a listening ear, a kind word, understanding and acceptance, as well as practical help.

Also, of immense help is to continue a bond with the deceased. Their personal items and their clothes can be kept for a long time, some given away and others kept, or never given away, there is no absolute right or wrong, only what is right for each individual person.

If some items are to be removed at some point, then the bereaved may begin that task and then abandon it when enough is enough, only to return repeatedly, when ready, maybe, unconsciously, needing to provoke the flow of warm, healing tears.

Keeping memories of the deceased can include any kind of object, physical or digital, such as letters, emails, texts, photos, phones, laptops, cards, hats, gloves, jumpers, perfume, aftershave, pajamas and jewelry and quite often the last thing that was used by that person. Other people may become concerned about what is kept, depending on what it is. It is somewhat perverse but there is usually no worry about keeping objects of monetary value. If you keep your mother's gold bracelet and wear it yourself, that's absolutely fine, but if you decide to keep her old slippers or well-worn armchair because they remind you of happy times spent together in front of the TV, then that may be seen as a bit peculiar or 'creepy'.

You may find yourself doing things or acting in a manner that is trying to make other people feel comfortable. You may find yourself putting on a stoic, public face and keeping your more obvious expressions of grief for private moments. It can be helpful to use our 'public face' to protect us from those thoughtless comments that may come our way, when we are particularly vulnerable, but it is also important not to change our behavior that is especially meaningful to us just to suit the needs of others. Do what feels right for you, but don't necessarily feel the need to tell other people what you choose to do.

Despair

Despair tends to occur when the numbness wears off, and the reality and permanence of death begins to penetrate. The bereaved person loses all hope of ever seeing that loved person again and that absence of a presence we once felt dear can seem unbearable. Even when bereaved people have strong religious beliefs that include being reunited in an afterlife, they still long to feel, hold, hear, embrace their loved one again now, in the present moment. Despair can last for a long time for some, it can come and go for others, but it won't remain as a constant feeling forever. It is natural to feel sadness, to yearn for the person we love to come back to us, for things to return to the normality that we once knew. Someone who shared part of our life is no longer there.

While you have little say in how you feel and how you will experience grief, you do have choices in how to deal with those feelings. Even in grief, you are not without resources. In acknowledging your grief and in recognizing that your emotions are normal and natural responses to loss, you can begin to cope with your feelings. Recovery from despair may be a slow process, but with support, acceptance, understanding, and by accessing our own internal resources, most of us will eventually experience hope again.

We may have to reassign roles or take on the duties that were previously performed by the loved one, but as we journey through grief, we begin to experience more good days compared to bad ones as we learn to accommodate the loss, start to rebuild our lives and make new social connections.

It may be helpful to you to know that most people who have suffered a devastating loss may never truly recover, but, over time, it becomes part of your life such that memories of your loved one are no longer all-consuming and disabling. We adapt and reconstruct a life without the loved one in it, but we never forget them.

Chapter Seven

GRIEF IS STRESSFUL

We are biologically designed to cope with stress on a short-term basis. We evolved to deal with a threat by removing it (fight), by escaping from it (flight), or by playing dead until it passed (freeze). But grief produces extended stress, not the short-term stress that we are designed to cope with, and this persistent stressful state contributes to auto stress disorders, such as anxiety, low mood, irritability, emotional ups and downs, poor sleep, poor concentration, wanting to be alone, recurrent dreams or flashbacks, all of which can be intrusive, unpleasant and make i t difficult to concentrate. This is because sustained stress increases levels of certain neurochemicals such as cortisol, corticotropin-releasing hormone, and adrenaline, and increases activation of the amygdala (our fear response center) and interferes with prefrontal brain areas (the brain's CEO), affecting our ability to maintain attention and focus and affecting our working memory. (Corticotropin-releasing factor regulates the immune responses in the central nervous system by mediating cytokine production and activation of peripheral immune cells.)

When most people think of grief, they think of sadness or emotional distress. Most people don't appreciate how physically stressful grief can feel. It is very common for people who are in prolonged stressful states, such as grief, to experience physical discomfort or pain. Stress is inflammatory, and when left untreated, it can cause a build-up of the same proteins that cause aches and pains when you have a cold or flu. These proteins, called cytokines, are natural defenses that the human body has evolved to produce to help support health. This aspect of the stress response can save your life if you are wounded or infected. But during a prolonged state of grief, this inflammatory response can make you feel quite unwell. The stress response system is not designed to be activated for prolonged periods without becoming impaired or creating problems for your mind and body. Cytokines can make you feel tired, achy, run down and lethargic, like having a cold but without the congestion.

A 2012 study in the American Heart Association journal, 'Circulation', showed that the danger of a heart attack was highest in the first 24 hours after the death of a loved one and that people with existing cardiovascular problems might be at particular risk. A follow up study carried out in 2014 showed that, for people aged 60 and older, there was more than twice the risk of a stroke or heart attack within 30 days of their partner's death, compared to people who hadn't suffered such a loss. Other research has linked grief to disrupted sleep, immune system changes and the risk of blood clots. You can see why prolonged grief, which affects around 10% of bereaved people, is a cause for concern as it carries with it serious health implications. For example, women who have been chronically depressed have also been found to have elevated levels of cortisol and decreased bone mineral density.

Basically, when we suffer a loss, our survival system can go into overdrive, causing disruptions to our sleep and concentration and making us feel tense, anxious, angry or depressed. If the brain's emergency response system is kept on high alert for prolonged periods by the upsetting thoughts that pass through our minds as we retrospect about past losses and anticipate future pain, then we can suffer the physical effects of excessive cortisol which is corrosive to many areas of the body.

During stress, cortisol acts to:

Increase heart rate.

Increase blood pressure.

Constrict blood vessels.

Decrease heart rate variability (increasing the risk of sudden death).

Increase cholesterol.

Increase adrenaline.

We are unlikely to be aware of elevated levels of the stress hormone cortisol as our daily response to grief usually falls short of the full physiology of the fight-flight response, our minds are too occupied with grief related concerns and we don't expect to feel well, in any case, as we grieve. But our elevated levels of cortisol can cause physical harm to organs and tissues, including elevated blood sugar (diabetes), elevated serum lipids (atherosclerosis), elevated stomach acid (peptic ulcers), osteoporosis, elevated blood volume (hypertension), and depressed immune function (opportunistic infections – grievers always seem to be more susceptible to colds and flu). These health problems are specific to the presence of cortisol, they are not linked to changes in the brain, and they are solely caused by the continued input of stress to the limbic (primitive) system. They will persist only for as long as the stress continues. They become of critical concern if the stress of grief proceeds to a state of prolonged helplessness when the physiology changes from a cortisol, endocrine reaction, which can be switched off, to an autonomic/freeze syndrome, (clinical depression), which is not so easily treated.

If our bodies are not quickly returned to normal, we are at greater than average risk of developing more serious health problems. As strange as it may seem, shedding tears of grief can help to reduce our vulnerability to infection because our tears contain healing and sedating chemicals.

The slightly technical description given above simply says that stress is damaging to our bodies as well as our minds and that grief produces an environment of persistent stress. The best way to reduce this stress is to talk to a caring listener, cry when you feel the urge, don't hold back your emotions, do something physically active whenever you can, take naps, a massage, a short trip out of the

house. There are many more suggestions in the later chapter about coping strategies.

Chapter Eight

UNUSUAL EXPERIENCES

M any people that I have counseled have reported feeling the deceased's presence and it is, in fact, a well-documented occurrence. There have been reports of familiar smells, hearing someone, feeling their touch, or even seeing them after they had died. Although sometimes disturbing, these experiences are usually comforting and tend to disappear within a few months.

Dreams of the deceased are common too and though most are quite straightforward, some can be less clear, more disturbing, and full of symbolism. Not all experiences are comforting either, especially if the relationship with the deceased was troubled or if their death was traumatic. Nightmares can be common under these circumstances.

If you have not had any unusual experiences or dreams associated with your loss, then that is quite normal too. Sometimes we long for such an experience to be able to feel a sense of connection.

Some people try to contact their deceased through mediums or spirit guides, but I would caution you first to explore and address the needs that underlie your desire for contact, and whether such an experience is appropriate to your own spiritual values. Some individuals offering these services may be sincere, but it is preferable to be cautious.

Most of these unusual experiences are common, comforting, and reaffirm a sense of connection. Research suggests that more than half of all grieving people report one or more of these experiences. Even so, we don't know much about them, and they occur unexpectedly. Most bereaved individuals find such experiences comforting, yet they are afraid to discuss them, fearing the reactions of others.

If you have any kind of unusual experience, it may help to find someone you know and trust and tell them about your experience. If your experience is troubling you, then it may be best to talk to a bereavement counselor.

Chapter Nine

GENDER DIFFERENCES IN GRIEF

M en and women tend to experience and express emotions differently, and so they tend to grieve differently too. This is due to biological differences and the socialization that occurs as we grow from childhood to adulthood.

Men are typically thought of as being less emotional than women. They feel the same intense pain and suffering as women do following a loss, but they don't show it. They suppress the outward manifestation of grief. Typically, Western society expects men to be strong and stoic, while women should be emotional and sensitive. Because of this, it is expected that many men will focus on what they think about their loved one's death, and many women will focus on how they feel about their loss. We can feel ashamed, guilty, or weak if we don't feel or act our part, according to our learned gender behaviors.

Over time, with successive generations, the socialization of girls and boys has been converging. Whilst gender differences remain within society, many people now hold non-stereotypical gender roles. Women are now active in the workplace, in occupations historically undertaken by men, and many men are now primary caregivers. These changes blur the lines of sex expectations and allow individuals to express themselves in a more authentic way, rather than being dictated by society. However, this is still a slow evolution.

Your gender may influence not only your grief but also how others relate to you. Although not always the case, men are often encouraged and expected to 'be strong' and restrain their emotions. Men will often have more difficulty in allowing themselves to move toward painful feelings than women do.

Women, though, can have a difficult time expressing feelings of anger. They may feel anger, but they may feel that expressing that anger is inappropriate for their gender. Men are usually quicker to respond with explosive emotions. Also, because men are expected to be self-sufficient, they will often find it difficult to accept outside support.

Crying and lamenting and publicly expressing feelings and emotions are usually stereotyped as being typically feminine responses, as is expressing emotions in front of other family members and friends who can relate to the mourner's grief over their loss. A typically feminine style of grieving involves the outward expression of grief. Public expressions of mourning, sadness and crying are all examples of expressing your grief. In outwardly expressing the effect that grief is having on them, women are also, subconsciously, signaling to others that they are in pain, that they are suffering and would appreciate being comforted by members of their social circle or support group as they mourn their loss.

In contrast, holding in your feelings is typically seen as a masculine trait. Men keep busy to avoid their feelings. They channel their feelings into actions, and they experience grief physically rather than emotionally. A man will often deal with loss by focusing on what's next on their to-do list or on other goal-oriented activities. They want to do things rather than to sit and talk about their feelings or to cry over their losses. You may well see a man spring into action by planting a memorial garden or by building a memorial bench or chiseling away at a memorial stone. These types of activities allow men the opportunity to do things that are directly related to their loss as they experience the impact of their grief.

Our society places a high value on what are considered to be the proper responses to grief following a loss. The traditional roles that men and women occupy can have a direct effect on how they grieve.

Incongruent Grieving

This is the term used to describe how heterosexual partners grieve differently after the death of a child. They appear to conflict in how they grieve and not to meet each other's expectations. In my counseling sessions with bereaved couples, I will often hear my female clients complain that their male partner is not really grieving or doesn't really care or is now 'over it' because he chooses not to talk about the loss. Male clients will often say that their partner is being over-emotional or isn't in control of themselves. Some men even feel angry because they are being told, "You don't care, you never show any emotion." Explaining that men grieve in one way, whilst women grieve in a different way can be of immense help and a relief to a bereaved couple, especially when they understand that there is a physical and cultural basis for the difference in male and female expressions of emotions.

Chapter Ten

RELATIONSHIPS

Bereavement, like any major life crisis, will often result in reviewing and changing your current relationships. There's a well known saying that 'you know who your real friends are when times get tough'. Grief has a way of bringing some friends closer and of moving some friends further away. In fact, some friends may simply 'disappear' from your life. You, yourself, will change too. The way that you look at life changes and your priorities change. Things that once seemed so important may no longer interest you; some acquaintances no longer show up in your life; complex relationships that brought conflict into your life are just not worth the effort; you no longer have the time or the energy for unreasonable and demanding people. Bereavement often brings about a 'clean sweep', an opportunity to start again, to assess what is important to you, and to spend time with the people who really matter.

In our grief, we are confronted with the impermanence of life, and we come to understand that it is fleeting and precious, and that no matter what amount of time we may have left, it is far too valuable to be wasted. But, before making any radical changes, it is worth reminding ourselves that it is us, the bereaved, who have changed, not others. You may find yourself making new friends, as well as keeping some of your old and cherished friends. It is worth remembering that new friends will get to know you as you are now. They will have no expectations or hopes that you will return to being your former self, unlike existing friends, who may be holding on to the belief that your new found self is a temporary one.

Bereavement often makes us become more, not less of who we really are. Many of us will become less inhibited, more assertive, and less likely to hold back on our thoughts and feelings. In grief, we can become quite outspoken. We may also become more prone to risk taking. The sheer pain of grief can override our concerns about what others may think. These changes may be welcomed by some around us but can become a cause of concern for others. It's worth remembering that going too far can cost us some of the

people closest to us, who may later become especially important to us.

Chapter Eleven

SEX AND GRIEF

Our gender will often influence the effect that grief has on our libido. Biology and socialisation influence our sexual interest and our sexual expression. Generally speaking, women's biology and socialisation lets them attain intimacy and express desire through verbal communication, sensitivity and affection, while men, on the other hand, because of their biology and socialisation, will often believe that intimacy can only be achieved through sex. These are generalizations. I have counselled women who have sought intimacy through sex and men who have sought intimacy through gentleness and affection. There are always exceptions to every rule.

Acute grief though, as a rule, complicates most people's normal sexual responses. It is quite common for both men and women to lose interest completely for a while, and even males who continue to be interested will often find their performance reduced. Temporary impotence or premature ejaculation is common in these cases. There are some, though, whose sexual desire increases rather than decreases, as they try to find some comfort and reassurance, and a distraction from the intense emotional pain of bereavement. Again, there are always exceptions to every rul e.

Within a relationship, when the loss is not experienced to the same degree by both partners, such as, when the parent of one of the partners dies, stability will usually return in a relatively brief period of time. But when a child dies, neither partner will have enough inner resources to take care of the other whilst trying to take care of themselves. Besides which, each partner will most likely need care and comfort in a different way, causing them to interpret each other's needs as being strange or abnormal. For example, if the man looks for comfort through sex, but his female partner feels physically and emotionally incapable of responding, they may distance themselves from each other, causing each of them to feel rejected or misunderstood, and consequently becoming critical of each other. She may see him as being self-centered and demanding, and he may see her as being cold and withholding. I have seen this many times in my years as a counselor.

Problems can arise, though, when one, or both of them, develop anxieties about resuming a sexual relationship. This usually happens because, either consciously or unconsciously they are trying to avoid more pain. After all, it was their sexual relationship that produced the child that they now mourn. Why take the risk of getting hurt again? When a child dies, women will often feel guilty, and somehow responsible, while men will often feel angry and blame someone else. The man's anger, though, can push his wife away, especially when her needs are for tenderness, comfort, and reassurance, but her withdrawal may make him feel rejected. It is easy in these circumstances to create a vicious circle which distances them from each other more and more. If the distance becomes too great, the relationship may well come to an end, just when they need each o ther most.

Distancing in a relationship isn't necessarily a bad thing though. Calling a time out, temporarily, can allow each partner to attend to their emotional needs without feeling the pressure to attend to their partner's emotional needs at the same time. Most bereaved people, when asked, say that they feel vulnerable, and, at times, inept, and they tend to lose some measure of self-esteem as a result. Those people who have previously experienced grief or trauma early on in their lives may regress to those earlier emotions and feelings, and experience even more vulnerability. It is important, therefore, that caring relatives and friends, or maybe a bereavement counselor, help to hold the relationship together by taking care of each individual separately, in the manner that best suits that individual, instead of them having to focus on their relationship while their resources are so desperately depleted.

Once both partners understand that sexual interest, or disinterest, is neither good nor bad, it 'just is', they can begin a dialogue that decreases the distance between them. Both partners are looking for comfort in their own individual way, struggling to survive, and with a bit of help, they may be able to learn how to meet some of their own needs in such a manner that they don't place unrealistic expectations on a relationship that is finding it hard going, with badly depleted resources. If a couple's sexual relationship continues to be out of balance for a protracted period, or begins to cause either partner unnecessary anguish, it may be best to look for professional counselling, preferably from someone who understands both relationship counselling and grief counselling.

Sexual 'acting out'

Sexually 'acting out' when someone close to a person is dying, or when the person is newly bereaved, is a well-documented phenomenon. It is usually a temporary phenomenon, quite often a once-only occurrence, although the behavior may shock the grieving person as well as others who are close to them. Guilt and remorse usually follow, with the grieving person asking themselves, "How could I do it, what was I thinking, how could I be so selfish, how could I do something that is so out of character for me?"

There are many possible explanations, and the behavior appears to be common. Sometimes it is just the need for physical contact, the need to be held and to hold, sometimes it is a reaction to the fear of death. Libido is life force, it is life affirming, the very antithesis of death. If you have experienced this kind of behavior and you regret it, it is important to understand that it is quite a common reaction to loss and forgive yourself instead of beating yourself up. If you are still unable to move on, talk to a trained bereavement counselor so that you can gain a more objective viewpoint.

Chapter Twelve

ALCOHOL AND OTHER DRUG USE

Most newly bereaved people find that their intake of alcohol and other drugs (such as nicotine, caffeine, analgesic painkillers, anti-inflammatories, tranquilizers) increases, usually on a temporary basis. The pain of grief is so intense and unremitting that most of us will do anything to experience some relief and anesthetize our feelings. Most of the physical discomfort comes from the adrenaline and cortisol that our bodies produce, as described previously. To combat these effects, Doctors may prescribe tranquilizers or sleeping tablets, or both, on a short-term basis. Taking sleeping tablets occasionally can help and taking a tranquilizer at times of anxiety, fear or panic can also help. Taking these medications allows us to feel more 'in control' of our grief, rather than feeling like we have no control over it whatsoever. But prolonged use may delay grief and can lead to tolerance of, and subsequent dependence on, the prescribed medication. The last thing we need as we grieve is another problem to deal with!

You might be prescribed antidepressants a few weeks after the death of someone you love if your profound sadness is diagnosed as depression. Based on more than twenty years of working with bereaved people of all ages and cultures, I think it is highly unlikely that anyone who hasn't suffered a depressive illness in the past will develop one as the result of a single event such as bereavement. But, if depression existed in the past, then symptoms may worsen in grief and may require the attention of your medical practitioner and/or counselor. Sometimes grief can trigger experiences from the past, especially those that did not receive adequate or appropriate attention at the time. This, in turn, can create complications that would require the need for professional help. If anything about your grief concerns you, including the way you use drugs of any kind to lessen your pain, then don't hesitate to see a grief specialist. People who understand grief will not judge your behavior.

Too much coffee can be problematic too. Coffee can cause agitation that can easily be interpreted as panic. Elevated levels of caffeine have been known to create a sense of doom that may tempt us to treat the symptoms with alcohol or tranquilizers to calm us down, especially if the panic occurs at bedtime and we are having difficulty sleeping. It is usually best to moderate caffeine intake and dissipate our agitation by doing something to burn up the energy. Physical activity burns off the adrenaline and taking our mind off our current situation allows the cortisol to metabolize to a manageable level. Tidying the house, cleaning out the garage, walking the dog, mowing the lawn or doing the ironing are all tasks that can tire us out, reduce agitation, and leave us feeling righteous rather than anxious.

Chapter Thirteen

WHY SLEEP IS IMPORTANT IN GRIEF

What Happens When We Sleep?

When we sleep, we alternate between two types of sleep. One is called REM sleep, which stands for rapid eye movement, also known as 'paradoxical sleep', because, although the body is sleeping, the brain is very active. REM sleep is when we dream. In REM sleep, our body is immobilized, but our eyes are moving around rapidly. The other type of sleep is simply called non-REM sleep. This is when you are completely asleep and are not dreaming. Non-REM sleep is 'deep sleep,' the most restful and restorative kind of sleep. You alternate between these two types of sleep throughout the night, but with periods of REM sleep lasting longer as the night wears on, producing the most vivid dreams as you get closer to waking up. You might wake up just before or just after each interval of REM sleep, as this is the period of sleep when your brain is most active. REM sleep takes up 20 – 25% of our sleep t ime.

Sleep, specifically REM sleep, is essential for us to heal our emotional wounds. The act of dreaming during REM sleep, and of dreaming of those emotional events which trouble us, is necessary to achieve resolution and keep our minds safe from the grip of anxiety and reactive feelings of depression.

Dreams and stress

In grief, our stress response is activated constantly throughout the day, and our brains interpret that as being in a persistently threatening environment. Because of this, our bodies produce, along with other chemicals, cortisol, adrenaline and noradrenaline. Noradrenaline is the brain's equivalent to the adrenaline that courses through the body and it is a stress-related chemical. Usually, during REM sleep, concentrations of this anxiety inducing chemical are shut off within the brain. This is done to ease the reprocessing of upsetting experiences in a calm dreaming environment, removing the emotional charge from our daily experiences.

Under normal circumstances, after a good night's sleep, we will usually wake up feeling better about whatever distressed us the previous day. That's because REM-sleep dreaming allows us to remember the details of important experiences, whilst, at the same time, dissolving the painful emotional charge that came with those experiences. You may have noticed that when you think back over your strongest emotional memories, they don't carry the same impact that they did at the time? You keep the memory, but without all, or most of, the visceral reaction that you felt at that time. That's because REM sleep dreaming dissolves away the emotion from the experience, leaving a narrative memory of the event, not an emotional one. In this way our dreams help us to discharge accumulated stress and return us to a normal functioning emotional state. For this reason, getting the right amount and quality of REM sleep is very important in helping us to process and resolve our grief.

In a depressive state, worrying and stress increase the intensity of REM sleep, causing it to start earlier on in the night and reducing the amount of deep, restorative sleep that we need to repair the brain and body. As intense dreaming continues throughout the night, the person wakes up feeling exhausted and lacking in motivation.

If, however, insomnia and nightmares prevent REM sleep from doing its job of calming the emotions of the previous day, the amygdala, the center of our survival instincts, is left in a heightened state of arousal. Thus, insufficient REM sleep leaves the amygdala much more reactive to emotionally charged events, which increases our overall stress and leads to difficulty maintaining intellectual control, leaving us at the mercy of our emotions.

For people who struggle to get enough sleep or are woken regularly by nightmares, a lack of effective REM sleep will lead to a build up of residual anxiety as it accumulates with time. For depressed individuals, though, because they worry too much, they create an overload of dreaming, and this overload of dreaming uses up so much energy in the brain that it leaves them feeling exhausted, no matter how long they have slept for. Fear, anxiety, anger, and many other emotions can obstruct effective REM sleep whilst worry, depression, loneliness, hopelessness can create too much REM sleep. There can be consequences for us either way.

Given the whole range of emotions that the bereaved have to endure, the importance of regularizing sleep patterns cannot be overstated. The right amount and quality of REM sleep will help to keep us from the grip of anxiety, fear, anger, worry, depression and a whole host of other emotions that may plague us as we adapt to our loss.

Adopting good sleep hygiene, trying to relax as much as is possible prior to sleep and perhaps using a hypnotic sleep recording or a mindfulness sleep routine can be of tremendous benefit to the bereaved as it all prepares the way for REM sleep to do its job.

Chapter Fourteen

GOOD SLEEP HYGIENE

Preparing yourself to sleep as best you can is referred to as having good sleep hygiene. It involves putting yourself in the best position you can to sleep well every night. This is achieved by optimizing your sleep schedule, creating a pleasant bedroom environment, and by adopting a daily and a pre-bed routine. Listed below are a handful of tips that can help with this, but they aren't rigid requirements. You can adapt them to your own individual circumstances and create your own sleep hygiene formula to enable the best sleep possible.

Create A Sleep Schedule

Having a regular, set schedule accustoms your brain and body to getting the full amount of sleep that you, as an individual, need.

On weekdays and on weekends, it is best, if possible, to wake up at the same time every day, because a fluctuating sleep schedule impedes you from getting into a regular rhythm of consistent sleep.

Although it can be tempting to skip a few hours of sleep in order to get more work or study done or to socialize, or exercise, it is important to treat sleep as the number one priority. Calculate a target bedtime based on the time that you want to wake up and then do your best to be ready for bed around that time each night.

If you need to alter your sleep times, try not to do it all in one go, because that can really throw your schedule out of kilter. It is best, instead, to make small, incremental adjustments of an hour or two so that you gradually settle into a new routine.

Naps can seem like a good way to recharge during the day, but they can interrupt your sleep at night. If you really need to take a nap, try to keep it relatively short and limited to the early afternoon.

Follow a Nightly Routine

Preparing for bed with a nightly routine can make it much easier to fall asleep when you want to.

Adopting the same routine each night, like putting on your pyjamas in the evening and brushing your teeth at a set time, will reinforce, in your mind, that it's time for bed soon.

Winding down thirty minutes before bedtime can put you in a more calm and relaxed state. Soft music, stretching a little, reading something light, and relaxation exercises all aid in preparing for a good night's sleep.

Try to avoid bright lights in the evening, as they can hinder the production of melatonin, which is a hormone that the body creates to facilitate sleep.

Try to create a device free 30 to 60-minute period each night before bedtime. It is well documented that phones, tablets, computers and laptops create mental stimulation that can be hard to switch off from and they also generate blue light that can affect the production of melatonin.

Instead of focusing on falling asleep, it's usually more productive to focus on relaxing. Meditation type relaxation techniques, regular, paced breathing, and other physical relaxation techniques can create the optimum mindset for bedtime.

You need to promote a healthy mental connection between being in bed and actually sleeping. So, if after 20 minutes you haven't fallen asleep, get up and stretch, read something light, or do something else that you find calming whilst in low light before trying again to fall asleep.

Cultivate Healthy Daily Habits

It's not just your bedtime habits that help in getting a good night's sleep. There are positive routines that you can adopt during the day which will support your circadian rhythm and keep sleep disruptions to a minimum.

Daylight, especially direct sunlight, is one of the key determinants of our circadian rhythms and will encourage quality sleep.

Regular exercise makes it easier to sleep at night too, especially outdoor exercise in the sunlight and, of course, there are many other health benefits.

Not smoking or, at least, cutting down on smoking really helps, as nicotine stimulates the body in ways that can disrupt quality sleep. It has been scientifically observed that smoking is correlated with many sleeping difficulties.

Alcohol can make it easier to fall asleep, but the effect wears off after a few hours and it then disrupts sleep as the night continues. Given that REM sleep lengthens as the night wears on, alcohol really interrupts our most effective periods of REM. To aid in quality sleep, it's best to moderate alcohol consumption and to avoid it later in the evening.

Cutting down on caffeine in the afternoon and evening is recommended because it's a stimulant. Caffeine can keep you hyped-up even when you want to rest, so it is best to avoid it later in the day.

Eating late, especially a big, heavy, or spicy meal, can mean that you're still digesting your food when it's time for bed. It's best to stop eating at least three hours before bedtime or to keep evening snacks on the lighter side.

Try to build a link in your mind between being in bed and sleeping. It's best to only use your bed for sleep, with having sex being the one exception, of course.

Optimize Your Bedroom

Creating a feeling of tranquility in the bedroom can be a really helpful part of good sleep hygiene.

What makes a bedroom inviting will vary from one person to another, but there are common ways to make it calm and disruption free.

A comfortable mattress and pillow are crucial to comfortable and pain-free sleep. So too are good quality sheets and blankets.

Bedroom temperature helps aid sleep, with cooler temperatures being preferable.

Using heavy curtains, effective window blinds or an eye mask to prevent light from interrupting your sleep is, to my mind, essential to quality sleep.

Creating a quiet sleep environment may involve the use of earplugs or a white noise machine or even a fan to drown out sounds that are bothersome.

Calming scents work well too. Lighter smells, such as lavender, may help to induce a calmer state of mind and cultivate a more positive space for sleep.

Chapter Fifteen

COPING STRATEGIES

As outlined earlier in this book, grief is a very personal experience, and the grieving process is unique to everyone, but there are some effects that are quite common. We have seen that the wave-like pattern of grief means that there may be periods of calm interspersed with periods of overwhelming emotions when a sudden event or comment triggers memories of the loved one. This section aims to provide some helpful strategies for coping with grief.

Talking about your loss is especially important and painful feelings and thoughts should not be bottled up as they can serve to fuel the immense stress that grief inflicts upon the bereaved. The sadness, depressive state and anxiety that go with the grieving process can be alleviated by giving expression to your grief.

For real recovery it is crucial that you face your grief and actively deal with it. The pain that being bereaved inflicts upon us needs to come out for us to start to process our loss and be able to learn to live with it.

When friends and family ask how they can help, let them know that just being there for you and listening is all that you need from them. It is of paramount importance that you are able to express your thoughts and feelings.

Try to expand your social network when you feel up to it or invite a friend or family member to lunch. This will certainly help you to recover from your loss, but avoid talking to people who you don't feel understand you, as this may not be helpful at this point.

Crying is incredibly important too. Just as you may need to talk about your loss, you may also need to find an outlet for suppressed emotions, so let the tears flow as this provides a way to release the stress hormones and toxins from the body. Although it is well known that women tend to cry far more often than men, it has been clinically proven that crying is a natural and healthy way to reduce emotional stress for all human beings, regardless of gender. So, if you ever feel like crying, please don't hold back, just go ahead and allow the pent-up emotions to pour out.

Allow yourself the time to grieve and feel sad. Although grief is not an illness, it can be likened, in many ways, to recovering from one, or to recovering from wounds that have been inflicted upon you. Time allows wounds to heal and repair. We recover from an illness over time. We cannot rush the healing process, but we can help it along, providing we don't overdo it.

Given that your recovery may take some time, don't put pressure on yourself to have to meet deadlines or commitments that you had previously made as people will understand.

Having said that, it is important that you do not stay passive for too long as research shows that people who were more prone to focusing inwards and not actively trying to lift their mood (by talking to others about their feelings or by taking up a more active life), were more prone to continue to feel depressed, or profoundly sad, 6 months later.

Join a support group

Some people find it extremely helpful to join a general support group where they can share their experiences with people who have gone through similar losses. These groups can provide comfort and support from fellow grievers, which can be a highly effective way to promote healing.

Self-help

Reading this book, and others, can be an important step in self-help. It has been proven that reading about grief can be extremely helpful and very therapeutic. It can be difficult to understand what is happening to your mind and body, especially if you don't have any other experience to compare it to, and bibliotherapy (reading self-help books) can be immensely helpful by providing information, support, and guidance.

Not exactly 'self-help', but allowing yourself to accept help from others can be extremely beneficial during these tough times. This is a difficult path to travel alone and all help, sympathetically and respectfully given, can enhance your ability to build a new life around the pain of loss.

What else can we do for ourselves?

Express yourself

Express yourself in whichever way you need to but be careful to only show the most vulnerable part of yourself to those you trust will not judge you or exploit your vulnerability.

Keeping a journal

Journaling can help some people. Keeping a diary of your thoughts and feelings gives you feedback about your progress.

Other forms of expression

There are many ways to express ourselves. Use whatever form of expression is familiar to you, something that expresses who you are. For example, painting, writing stories or poetry, dancing, gardening, walking or running, working, taking courses, cooking, playing sport, going to the gym, playing music, attending concerts, doing yoga, practicing martial arts. It is important though not to overdo things, as getting overtired can cause us to regress and to begin to feel overwhelmed. We just need enough tiredness to help us to sleep better.

Self-Care

We need to eat well, preferably simple, healthy food, and to have consistent exercise, gentle or more physically demanding, depending on your nature. The point is to ensure that we are breathing properly and using up adrenaline.

We need sunlight, at least ten minutes each day, if possible. Sunlight touching our eyelids changes our biochemistry and helps to prevent sadness becoming depression.

We need to factor in change; simple changes on a daily, weekly or monthly basis, that prevent us from slipping into a rut. Change might be as simple as finding a new route to work, school, wherever, one that doesn't bring back too many painful memories. Perhaps doing something nice for yourself on the way home.

Self-indulgence

Self-indulgence includes some or all of the things already mentioned, like sunlight or tasty, wholesome food. The importance of nutrient dense food is generally understood but the importance of sunlight is usually not so well understood. Sunlight not only changes our biochemistry but feels warm, gentle and soothing— just what we need right now.

Have a relaxing, nurturing massage. Buy something new to wear, or indulge your senses; sight, sound, touch, taste, smell. Find something beautiful, rousing, intriguing or soothing to look at; try a new perfume, aftershave, soap or shampoo; watch a movie or a TV series; listen to sounds that don't irritate you but soothe and relax you; try to cook or eat something different; and touch something that feels soft and sensuous.

You don't have to wait until you feel like doing any of these things for them to be effective. Just do them and the effect will follow.

Self-indulgence doesn't have to be expensive or time consuming either, all you need is a simple reminder that you are important.

Appetite

Most people's appetite decreases in the early days after bereavement, and tastes can change. Snacking is usually better than trying to eat a full meal. Snacking on things like fruit, nuts, yogurt, soup and salad. A multi-vitamin capsule is usually a good idea too, until normal eating is restored.

Writing - journal, email or letters

Don't let yourself be pressured into writing because someone else thinks it is a good idea. Writing only helps if it is something you do naturally. It can be especially useful in the middle of the night when you can't sleep, and friends are not available. At these times you can pour your thoughts and feelings out onto a page, whether it is a physical page or a digital page, whether that is in a journal, a letter or an email to an understanding friend or relative. Worries, concerns, and to-do lists can also be put on paper or on a 'to do' or task management app. Externalizing our thoughts is a decluttering exercise that helps to ease an already overloaded inner system.

The Art of Distraction

It is often said in bereavement counseling that learning to live with grief is largely about the 'art of distraction'. Whenever we experience emotional pain, it can be very helpful to stay with it just long enough to understand its source, identify its triggers, express whatever we feel we need to express in whichever way feels right to us, and then distract ourselves by doing something physical until we restore normal breathing. It is best to choose an activity that usually gives you pleasure, something that shifts your attention from your internal world into the external world. It has the effect of dispelling the dark emptiness of grief before it gets a foothold. There's an emptiness and a loneliness about grief that can settle into our very bones.

Identifying and expressing our pain, quickly followed by physical distraction is the best way of warding this off.

Bereavement counseling

The question many people ask themselves is – "Do I need grief counseling?"

If you think it might help, then there is no harm in attending just one appointment and making your mind up from there. People often think that they have to be in terrible shape before going to a counselor, very much like not calling the doctor unless your symptoms are unbearable or really worrying, but there isn't a particular level of intensity that you must be experiencing before calling a counselor.

Counseling can be helpful, even you are feeling pretty 'okay', as it helps you to explore your experiences in a supportive, confidential, and non-judgmental environment and counselors can provide what we call psychoeducation (an explanation of the psychological processes of grief – basically, what's happening to you) and help you identify coping strategies and resources for dealing with a wide range of stressors.

When grief is repressed because of trauma or because the bereaved has little support, other problems will often appear. Many individuals and families who come to therapy present with problems that seem to have nothing to do with bereavement, but the source of their problems often turns out to be an unprocessed loss. For example, I have counseled many people about drug and alcohol addiction that was ultimately traced to the death, years earlier, of someone they were close to. Similarly, when treating anxiety disorders and/or depression, it is not uncommon to uncover unresolved issues around a past bereavement. These losses can be carried around unrecognized but deeply felt for years before emerging as triggers for the current sense of discomfort.

Professional counseling should always have the goal of enabling individuals to heal themselves. The idea being to develop the skills needed to aid in coping with grief and to prepare for future times of grief. Therapy is not a form of dependency; it is a self-empowerment that equips us with the skills to resolve our pain ourselves. Any therapeutic treatment needs to be capable of being self-applied, have rapid results, and be easy to use, ultimately, without the guidance of a therapist.

Stay Active

Try to stay active as much as you can. Engaging in any physical activity is incredibly beneficial. Regular exercise could include running, cycling, walking, going to the gym, playing golf, but also activities such as gardening, fishing, or any outdoor hobby.

Remembering your loved ones

Birthdays, anniversaries, seasonal holidays and other occasions that remind you of your loved one can be particularly painful. Talk to family and friends about how you feel about these significant dates, as they may have suggestions. Try to think about introducing new traditions or new rituals to mark certain special occasions.

It can be helpful to put together a photo album, either a physical album or a digitized album that can be held in secure cloud storage, or both. It is also quite common to plant a tree or to buy or construct a bench in memory of your loved one.

If your loved one sponsored a particular cause, foundation, or charity, then you might think about continuing that sponsorship or activity, in some capacity, to honor their memory.

Express Yourself creatively

Writing or blogging can be a wonderful way to express yourself creatively.

The act of writing a letter or an email, even if you never send it, can be incredibly therapeutic and allows you to release your emotions, helping to bring clarity to the pain you are going through.

Other creative outlets might include drawing or painting, candle making, origami, wood carving, making jewelry, knitting, crocheting, baking and many, many others. An online search will quickly reveal countless creative ways to help you to relax and increase your sense of control.

Most important of all, avoid using chemicals to dull your feelings.

Trying to suppress your feelings with alcohol, medication or illicit drugs will only have the effect of keeping you in a depressed state for much longer. Eventually, one way or another, you will have to come to terms with your grief.

Take care of your physical health

As well as eating healthily and exercising regularly, good sleep is of paramount importance.

Grief takes enormous physical as well as emotional energy. It is incredibly draining and affects our whole nervous system. A combination of exercise, rest, eating properly and quality sleep are essential to recovery from grief.

If you are having difficulty with your appetite, then try to eat smaller portions of healthy foods with plenty of fiber rather than full meals. Avoiding processed food can be helpful too, as they can cause you to become irritable and suffer fatigue and mood swings.

If you are finding it difficult to sleep, then try to take small naps or try to relax by listening to some music with your eyes closed. There are hundreds of sleep hypnosis recordings available online that can be incredibly helpful in getting a good night's sleep and a professional hypnotherapist can create a tailor-made recording which focuses on your specific issues.

A massage can help you to relax, physically and mentally, and helps to reduce blood pressure.

If you are struggling more than you think you should be, then look for some professional help as a therapist can help with tools and techniques to support you and help you to come to terms with your loss. Grief counselors can offer a safe and confidential space to explore, talk about and make sense of your feelings in a non-judgmental way.

Grief counseling doesn't have to be undertaken on a long-term basis, as quite often people find that they can cope well after just a few sessions. Trying it out for just one session is certainly worth it and can't hurt.

Your doctor may also be able to recommend a therapist who specializes in grief support.

Chapter Sixteen

ACCOMMODATING LOSS

With time, your ability to think clearly and logically will gradually return. New routines emerge, and you may be able to make plans for the future. Bear in mind, the future may simply mean next week, but just being able to acknowledge that there is a future is a big step. There are often practical problems to address, like balancing the finances, paying the bills, tackling household chores. You may experience low energy and low mood for a while, making it difficult to get completely back on track, and there can be difficulty retaining information. Memory loss is very common, and many people may struggle to read books for any length of time in the first year. Children often have difficulty concentrating at school. At some point, usually as you enter the second year, there is a sense that order is emerging from the chaos, but if not, it can be helpful to see a bereavement counselor.

Keeping up with social connections is vital to regaining that sense of equilibrium and may involve the need to pretend that all is well for a while, even if all is not well. Do things with others as much as you are able, and act as though you are enjoying yourself. Bit by bit, small sensations of pleasure will emerge, even if short lived. Guilt may rear its head from time to time when you find yourself laughing for a moment, or having a good time, and then suddenly remembering the person who has died.

You may be quite hard on yourself by saying or thinking things like "How can I laugh when they are dead?" "Does this mean I stopped caring?" "Does this mean that I didn't love them as much as I thought I did?" "How selfish of me!" You may want to feel intense pain again to reassure yourself of your connection with the person you love. If this happens, reread the section of this book on guilt and how to cope with it.

Your grief and sense of loss may never diminish, but your life, over time, will grow around it. Your grief will always be there, sometimes you will be acutely aware of it and at other times you will barely notice it, but it will always be a part of your life. As time passes, life expands around our loss, making it a smaller proportion of our everyday reality without ever diminishing its importance. It's just that we naturally grow around our grief.

Over time, you will have new experiences, try new things, meet new people, visit new places and begin to find some moments of enjoyment. These moments will probably, slowly, become more frequent, and the grief that you felt will no longer be as dominant as it once was.

The idea of moving on from or forgetting our loved ones is one of the most problematic parts of grieving, but it is perfectly normal for grief to remain a part of your life. People who haven't experienced grief think that it has an endpoint, but those of us who have lost someone that we love know that there is no final cut off point for our feelings.

Someone might say to you, "I'm glad to see you're feeling better now", rather like getting over a bad cold, or you may hear someone say, "I don't think they ever got over the loss of their loved one ". People have this idea that grief is about 'closure', as though you, one day, simply close the cover on the book of grief as you've reached the end. Phrases like these imply that there will come a moment when the grief is over, done, finished, and, if it isn't, then we are made to feel like there's something wrong with us. But there isn't. There really isn't. We move forward with our lives, but we take our loved ones with us, we don't leave them behind.

Chapter Seventeen

WHAT HAPPENS IF THERE IS NO IMPROVEMENT?

There is no specific timetable for the process of recovering from a loss. Everyone is different and it cannot be overstated that the experience and symptoms of physical and emotional stress are unique to each person and for each loss. The timing and order of the recovery process will differ for each and every individual.

A lot will depend on how readily you are able to:

Accept and process the reality and finality of the loss

Permit yourself to experience the pain

Learn to cope with the reality of the loss and its consequences

Make plans for the future and develop new relationships and friendships

Most people adapt to loss after 6-12 months. Gradually the pain of their feelings lessens, and they find it possible to gain perspective on what happened, what it means to them, and they begin to move forward in life.

Grief changes from an all-consuming sadness to an integrated form in which the sadness and yearning become more subdued.

Put simply: you do not get over your loss, you learn to live with it as your life grows around it. People expect that grief reduces in size and intensity over time, whereas, in reality, the impact of grief and our attachment to the deceased remain the same. Our grief doesn't diminish, but our lives expand around it as we have new experiences, meet new people, and begin to find moments of pleasure again. Slowly, these moments become more frequent, as our lives grow around our grief.

The grief doesn't, necessarily, disappear, and it will probably always be there, in the background, even growing a little bigger at difficult times, but it no longer dominates your life as it once did.

For some people, though, the feeling of loss persists or even intensifies, and there is no improvement.

There may still be:

A persistent longing for the deceased person

A general sense of purposelessness

Continued difficulty accepting the loss

Anger at the death

Difficulty taking up new activities or resuming day-to-day routines

If this happens you may have complicated grief or prolonged grief disorder.

Around 10% of grieving people experience complicated grief, sometimes called persistent complex bereavement disorder. If you feel stuck in your grief and suspect that you may not be able to re-engage with life, then please seek professional help as soon as you can from a specialist who has experience in complicated grief as the painful emotions involved can be so long lasting and severe that you have trouble recovering from the loss and resuming your life.

The most worrying aspect of complicated or prolonged grief disorder is that 4% of individuals who suffer from this disorder go on to take their own life. Medical research has found that targeted, trauma-focused, psychological treatment is extremely helpful, particularly Cognitive Behavioural Therapy (CBT), Eye Movement Desensitisation and Reprocessing (EMDR), and Exposure Therapy. There are also 2 medications that many doctors recommend, which are used to treat PTSD in adults. They are; paroxetine and sertraline.

Paroxetine and sertraline are both a type of antidepressant known as selective serotonin reuptake inhibitors (SSRIs).

Alongside or instead of medication, targeted, trauma-focused, psychological treatments can help you regain a sense of control over your life by:

Teaching you skills to address your symptoms

Helping you think better about yourself, others and the world

Learning ways to cope if any symptoms arise again

Treating other problems often related to traumatic experiences, such as depression, anxiety, or misuse of alcohol or drugs

You don't have to try to handle the burden of complicated grief or prolonged grief disorder on your own, there is medication and tried and tested therapy that can be of immense benefit. Therapeutic approaches usually involve revisiting and talking about the deceased, working through the emotions that arise and developing strategies for coping.

The most important feature of grief is not to let it paralyze your life and stop you from ever living again and finding peace. It is important to take these steps to move through your grief, so that you can once again find happiness.

Chapter Eighteen

TESTING FOR MAJOR DEPRESSION EPISODE

The possibility of grief developing into clinical depression is one of the most worrying aspects of bereavement. As stated previously, clinical depression is highly unlikely for individuals with no previous history of depression who have experienced a single bereavement event. But for those with any previous experience with depression and for those who experience traumatic loss, multiple losses or who begin to experience complicated grief, it should certainly be of concern. Written below is a kind of short test that should be taken periodically to help to determine if you should be looking for professional help in your grief.

It should be of serious concern if five (or more) of the following symptoms have been present during the same two-week period and if they represent a change from previous functioning.

At least one symptom of the five or more symptoms is:

(a) depressed mood, or

(b) loss of interest or pleasure.

1. Depressed mood most of the day, nearly every day, as indicated by either your own subjective report e.g., feeling sad or empty or if that is an observation made by others e.g., appears tearful.

With children and adolescents, this can be an irritable mood.

2. A notably reduced interest in or pleasure from all, or almost all, activities most of the day, nearly every day (as indicated by either your own subjective observation or observation made by others).

3. Significant weight loss when not dieting or weight gain (e.g., a change of over 5% of body weight in a month) or decrease or increase in appetite nearly every day.

Note: In children, failure to make expected weight gains.

4. Insomnia or hypersomnia (excessive daytime sleeping) nearly every day.

5. Psychomotor agitation or retardation nearly every day (observable by others, not merely subjective feelings of restlessness or being slowed down).

Psychomotor retardation includes slowed speech, decreased movement, and impaired cognitive function (trouble remembering things, making decisions, concentrating).

Psychomotor agitation includes movements that serve no purpose, like pacing around the room, tapping your fingers or toes, or talking rapidly.

6. Fatigue or loss of energy nearly every day.

7. Feelings of worthlessness or excessive or inappropriate guilt (which may be delusional) nearly every day (not merely self-reproach or guilt about being sick).

8. Diminished ability to think or concentrate, or indecisiveness, nearly every day (either by subjective account or as observed by others).

9. Recurrent thoughts of death (not just fear of dying), recurrent suicidal ideation without a specific plan, or a suicide attempt or a specific plan for committing suicide. More often than not thinking, 'is this what life is all about?'

If you find that you experience five or more of these symptoms, and one of those is either depressed mood or loss of interest or pleasure, then it is very important that you consult a medical doctor and consider professional mental healthcare support. Clinical depression is different to feeling depressed about the loss of a loved one. Clinical depression rarely recedes of its own accord and can have serious long term consequences.

Chapter Nineteen

HELPING SOMEONE ELSE WHO IS GRIEVING

We have now looked at some of the most common 'symptoms' of grief, the process of grieving and the various tools available to aid in the recovery process, but what happens if someone we care about is grieving?

The tools and techniques we looked at previously can also be applied to help you support a grieving family member or friend.

Rather than being too worried about what to say or do for someone who is grieving or being concerned that you might say the wrong thing, you can instead provide them with your time and support. Offering a listening ear instead of talking and running the risk of saying the wrong thing is the best thing that you can do for them. Try to listen to them in an attentive, compassionate and empathetic way.

Never push someone into talking if they don't feel comfortable about doing so but let them know that you are there to listen to them should they want to. You will find that the bereaved person benefits immensely just from having their loss acknowledged.

You should keep your own conversation to a minimum and simply ask:

"Do you feel like talking?"

"I am not sure what to say but I want you to know that I care."

"Tell me what I can do for you."

If conversation is difficult then just sitting in silence and squeezing their hand or giving them a comforting hug can be enough.

Be aware that some statements may not be helpful at all, so please avoid saying things like:

"You should move on with your life."

"He or she is in a better place."

"It is fate or God's will."

Offer practical help, when a person is grieving, as they may find it difficult to ask for help.

You could offer them practical support such as helping with funeral arrangements during the early stages, doing the shopping or other errands, helping with household chores or childcare support or going with them somewhere.

Rather than simply asking what you can do for them, you could instead be more specific and say, "I am going to the shops later; can I get you anything?"

Providing them with ongoing support

Given that the grieving process varies considerably for each person and that some recover faster than others, it would be wise to bear in mind that your grieving friend or family member may need your ongoing support for a long time after the death.

Stay in regular contact with them, drop by or send a message or card to let them know that you are thinking of them.

It is well known that receiving cards or messages with a few kind words can help someone who is feeling depressed or experiencing low mood to recover much faster.

Give them the time they need to process their grief and try not to hurry things along as it may take some months or even years to fully recover.

Don't get impatient or agitated that you are not gaining any fun or benefit from the relationship.

Good friends or family members will be there for each other through good times and bad.

Be alert to signs of complicated grief

In the last chapter we looked at grief which does not appear to be improving even after a considerable time. If you believe this applies to your friend, then this may well be a sign that the person is suffering from prolonged grief disorder or complicated grief.

You may need to encourage them to look for professional help, particularly if there are warning signs such as alcohol or drug abuse or talking about dying or suicide.

If you find it difficult to raise your concerns, you could try telling them that you are worried that they aren't eating or sleeping, and that, perhaps, they should look at getting professional help.

Try to find a grief specialist and help them to set up an appointment. Always try to go with them to ensure that they attend the appointment. Seeking professional help as quickly as possible is important, because left untreated, complicated grief can lead to life-changing health issues, clinical depression and even suicide.

Chapter Twenty

GRIEF AND THE INTERNET

Digital legacies

The Internet, and particularly social media have changed society completely. Our experience of bereavement has been significantly affected too. There is now an added layer of complexity to the process of grieving, not only because there is often a digital legacy to consider but because handling online accounts, subscriptions and information can also increase our emotional anguish significantly.

Gaining access to bank accounts, removing other online accounts, closing subscriptions, and managing or deleting social media accounts can be both time consuming and emotionally overwhelming. The digital world is such a new and rapidly expanding area, but it can be confusing and legally challenging. Each organization has its own rules, and countries vary as to their treatment of online content after death. A further complication is the fear of losing data such as emails, text messages, digital photographs or video. Online backups and storage solutions are available to the bereaved, to preserve their precious digital inheritance. In theory, digital legacies are no different to inheriting filing cabinets full of paperwork, photos and videos, except that the deceased might not have had legal ownership of some of them.

To appreciate the scope of increasing numbers of online platforms, these can include social media platforms like Facebook, Twitter, Instagram, and LinkedIn, media sharing platforms like YouTube, Spotify, and Vimeo, online learning platforms, online communities, virtual worlds, backup storage for the content of phones, tablets, laptops, computers, online creative sites for music, online banking, email accounts, online shopping accounts, and many more. The full list is growing rapidly as we become more digitalised. Some of the content may be copyright protected and remain the property of the deceased, but that does not automatically ensure there are inheritance rights. Some of the content is owned by the online service provider, and will not pass to the next of kin, and that which does pass to the next of kin will likely require several documents to prove the death and the right to ownership as inheritance.

The more mature platforms have departments that are dedicated to helping the bereaved, whilst the newer platforms may still be developing and standardizing their procedures. Standardized, accepted international practice and laws will, no doubt, normalize over time but in the meantime the complications should be acknowledged.

If you do not feel up to handling the complexities that dealing with digital legacies involves, it may be best to ask a tech savvy friend or family member to help you. It is best to anticipate, too, that this process is likely to bring up some strong emotions. Many aspects of people's lives, their cherished memories, hopes and dreams, are, in part, housed online and it can be an emotional minefield having to transfer ownership and close down accounts and subscriptions.

The Hierarchy of Mourning

While it is more obvious in physical situations, the 'hierarchy' of mourners may not be as clear in the case of social media. The family, the 'chief mourners', may feel they should have complete control over the messaging online. However, other people may post without understanding that this dynamic exists. Social cues, for instance, are clear when we are interacting at funerals: immediate family sits at the front and those with the 'lesser' relationships sit or stand at the back. Within the online world, these cues are not so obvious.

Online bereavement étiquettes

Social media is a powerful medium for spreading the word and for public displays of emotion. The immediate family though can be easily offended by posts that they have not sanctioned. In the absence of a specific memorial website, private messaging may be more appropriate for expressions of grief until a precedent has been set by the digital inheritor.

Tagging the deceased person in posts may appear on the family's and friends' feeds, which could cause distress. The younger generation may not be as aware of these issues as the pre-internet generation, because they have grown up within a publicly expressive world.

Dedicated Online Memorial Sites

Prior to the Internet, memorials were restricted to physical objects, such as headstones and notices in local newspapers. These days, though, memorialization can include dedicated online memorial sites or social media pages. There are many sites worldwide that are set up to enable the bereaved to create a dedicated memorial page to their loved one, but families may have differing opinions as to what is proper content for an online memorial, what is not, and how to deal with the inherited legacy. Another complication is that anyone can post anything online, without consultation or consent. This can be particularly problematic with social media sites, and there have been stories of parents learning about the death of their child through a post on a social media site.

As technology evolves, the web of digitalisation will become ever more embedded within everyday life. This means the internet will become increasingly more important when it comes to legacy planning, dying, grieving, meaning making, and continuing bonds with the deceased. This is a complex area that is still developing and evolving legally, and which can cause confusion and added stress for the bereaved. I'm afraid that, in many cases, these issues will need to be thought about carefully and,

perhaps, discussed with other family members and close f
riends.

Digital immortality

There are several companies that provide services which
claim to provide an eternal avatar of a person. They claim
the thoughts and stories of someone can be preserved and
perpetuated for eternity. Whether these services support
the bereaved or prolong their grief (in the case of the cre-
ation of an avatar of the deceased) will depend on individual perspective. Death is final, grief is normal, and
continuing bonds with the deceased is normal, so the in-
troduction of technology in this area will need to be ethical
and considered.

Online support

An Internet search will quickly reveal many individuals
worldwide who write about their own, or other people's
individual grief experiences. Some of these may be helpful,
but caution should be exercised not to 'benchmark' or
compare your grief with theirs because every grief experience is unique to the individual. Many people give advice
that may apply to them personally, or others they know,
but the information may not be appropriate for someone
else.

CONCLUSION

We grieve for many different reasons, and we all grieve in different ways.

There are no right or wrong ways of experiencing grief although some thoughts and actions after suffering a loss can be more helpful than others and there are many ways that we can hasten the 'healing' process.

Maintaining a strong social support network, undertaking physical activities, developing new routines, taking up creative hobbies, giving yourself the time you need to grieve, being compassionate to yourself, attending support groups and seeing a professional grief specialist can all help with the emotional and physical symptoms of grief.

There may be times when we feel we have moved forward in our lives but a sudden or unexpected event or a special occasion, piece of music or particular place may bring back memories of the loss and the grief comes surging back like a tidal wave. Revisit the coping strategies in this book at any time you feel the need and remember that time is the greatest healer of all.

It may be helpful to consider that the best way we can respect the loss of a loved one is to live and fulfill the lives that they would have wanted for us. They surely would not want us to spend the remainder of our lives grieving. They would have wanted us to let go of the pain and get back to finding happiness again as soon as possible.

Grief impacts every fiber of our being. It cannot be stressed enough that it is important to express whatever we feel the need to express and not be restricted by the needs of others. We all need compassionate and non-judgemental support, and we all need whatever time it takes to rebuild a shattered world.

Thank you for purchasing this book, I hope it was helpful for you during this most profoundly distressing time.

Please leave a review for this book on amazon as I would like to hear your comments and feedback.

Grief Resources

Visit Addison at: https://www.copingwithgrief.net

Contact: https://www.copingwithgrief.net/contact/

Grief Help:

Free Grief Help 8 Week Course : https://www.coping-withgrief.net

Free Book "Grief, What You Should Know" Available For Download: https://www.copingwithgrief.net